D0581739

Recipes From Cornwall
Food Ideas from Cornwall's Top Chefs

Published by Atmosphere
Willis Vean
Mullion Cornwall TR12 7DF
England
Tel 01326 240180

All images Copyright Bob Croxford 2007
All recipes Copyright the respective chefs 2007
Book Design and typography by Bob Croxford Copyright Atmosphere 2007
Printed and bound in Italy

ISBN 978-0-9543409-9-5

With very special thanks to Karen Forster for Research, Liaison and getting this book together.

Many of the pictures in this and other Atmosphere books are available as large photo prints to frame. For details of sizes and prices see www. atmosphere.co.uk/prints.html

INTRODUCTION

Thirty years ago Cornwall was almost a culinary desert. Very few restaurants excited the palates of food critics and reviewers. A few early pioneers have now been joined by many other chefs devoted to good food and good ingredients. Now we have a county almost bursting with catering pride. Hardly a week goes by when Cornish restaurants aren't mentioned by the glossy magazines. This new activity is backed up by a resurgent interest from farmers and fishermen in producing the finest ingredients. Inspired by the raw materials available the chefs in this small book produce unique and tasty food.

Andy Carr, THE BAKEHOUSE
Chapel Street, Penzance, 01736 331331
The Bakehouse is a bright and colourful restaurant with a flower-filled courtyard. Often features exhibitions of famous local artists. Andy is a well known local chef using best of Cornish produce. 'Great flavours, wonderful presentation and proper portions.' (**Page 15, 60**)

Grant Nethercott, ALBA RESTAURANT
The Old Lifeboat House, St Ives, 01736 797222
Grant worked with Gary Rhodes and in a 2 Michelin-starred restaurant in the South of France before moving to Cornwall where he has worked for the past 13 years. His cooking is fish biased. The restaurant overlooks the stunning harbour of St Ives and the bay beyond. Contemporary decor in an old life-boat house. AA Seafood Restaurant of the Year. Two AA Rosettes.
(**Page 50**)

Nigel Parry, THE BEACH RESTAURANT
Sennen Cove, 01736 871191
"Its about combining simplicity and local ingredients with breathtaking scenery". Highly commended for its architectural design boasts large terrace to relax and enjoy panoramic view of beautiful and unspoilt beach of Sennen. Local family business established in 1959. Daily specials take advantage of finest seasonal ingredients from seafood to Cornish-reared meat. (**Page 29**)

Tony Henshaw, EDEN PROJECT
Bodelva, St Austell, 01726 811911
*Hugely successful eco tourist attraction. Ethos of sustainable living so great interest in use of food and effect on planet. Local sourcing policy aims to showcase the best of local produce and aims to transport produce as short a distance as possible. Don't knowingly include GM ingredients. Head Chef Tony Henshaw plans menus with local products in mind. (**Page 46**)*

Ben Harmer, THE EDGE BAR & RESTAURANT
6 New Road, Port Isaac, 01208 880090
*As name states, stands on edge of North Cornish coast in historic fishing village. Wood burning stove and views out to sea and Tintagel Castle from light and airy restaurant. Ben previously worked at Rick Steins. (**Page 12**)*

Kyan Hooper, ELEMENTS
Widemouth Bay, Bude, 01288 352386
*Set on cliff tops of North Cornwall. Premier surf hotel, cafe bar and restaurant. Recently redesigned and refurbished. Fresh, locally sourced 'real' food served throughout day. (**Page 40**)*

Neil Haydock, FIFTEEN CORNWALL
On the Beach, Watergate Bay, 01637 861000
Executive Head Chef resigned as Chef de Cuisine
at the world-renowned Sandy Lanes resort in
Barbados to work at Fifteen. With top-class
produce to hand, the food at Fifteen is simply
prepared with care and passion. Magnificent
facilities, top-class kitchen - open plan so really
*feel part of the restaurant. (**Page 21**)*

Jude Kereama, KOTA
Harbourhead, Porthleven, 01326 562407
Previously at The Smokehouse, Porthleven.
Modern seafood, meat and game - all organic.
New Zealand Chef Jude fuses the flavours of
European and Asian cultures in his globally
*inspired menu. (**Page 43**)*

Paul McKenna, FISTRAL BLU BAR
Headland Road, Newquay, 01637 879444
Spectacular views, unique sunsets, award-
winning building, fine dining. The perfect Cornish
Bistro. Open all day for tapas, light bites, fresh
local seafood, seasonal meat, delicious desserts.
*(**Page 49**)*

Anton Buttery, LANGMANS RESTAURANT
3 Church St, Callington, 01579 384933
Great gourmet experience offered with 6-course
tasting menu showcasing modern British
cooking using fresh, local produce. All food
prepared in-house from bread rolls to petit
fours. 2 AA Rosettes. Regular Award winners in
Cornwall Tourist Board's Restaurant of the Year
*category. (**Page 16**)*

Dan Zackey, MILL HOUSE INN
Trebarwith, Tintagel, 01840 770200
Formerly 18th century corn mill now provides first class food and board as a traditional inn. Features in Alastair Sawday's Special Places. Set in own 7 acre wooded valley and garden.
(Page 23)

Keir Meikle, THE NAVY INN
Lower Queen St, Penzance, 01736 362104
Previously worked at Savoy and with Antony Worrall Thompson. Chef proprietor. Relaxed informal dining. Award-winning menu. Focus on local fish, shellfish and organic meats. Exceptional value. (Page 34)

Michael Smith, PORTHMINSTER BEACH CAFE
Porthminster Beach, St Ives, 01736 795352
Australian chef. Previously worked in Australia,
London and Edinburgh. Specialises in seafood.
Mediterranean menu with a modern Aussie twist.
Stunning position right on beach taking
advantage of special magical St Ives light. Fish
landed in the morning is served at lunchime.
*(**Page 58**)*

Paul Ripley, RIPLEY'S
St Merryn, Padstow, 01841 520179
One of only 3 Michelin Star restaurants in
Cornwall. Was head chef at Rick Stein's Seafood
Restaurant for 10 years. Excellent service, excellent
*food. Specialises in seafood dishes. (**Page 39**)*

Ann Long, THE RISING SUN
St Mawes, 01326 270233
There are views of the Roseland Peninsula from
Colonial style restaurant with glassed-in terrace.
Ann is the only woman Master Chef of Great
Britain in the Westcountry. Specialises in new
and innovative dishes using quality Westcountry
*produce. (**Page 19**)*

Grady Boone, REVIVAL
Charlestown Harbour, 01726 879053
2 AA Rosettes. Within Grade II former Rashleigh
Fishery. Open to eaves - light and airy.
American chef produces strong, bold flavours
with a delicate touch. (Page 24)

Nigel Tabb, TABB'S
85 Kenwyn St, Truro, TR1 3BZ
Previously at the famed Tabb's at Portreath, the
stylishly re-furbished Tabb's Truro opened in 2005.
A proper fine dining experience, Nigel uses top
class ingredients in his weekly changing menu
where everything is made on the premises. Two
AA Rosettes. (Page 53)

Dez Turland, ROYAL DUCHY HOTEL
Cliff Road, Falmouth, 01326 319420
The Terrace Restaurant. Fabulous setting looking
out over Gyllyngvase Beach and Falmouth Bay.
Relaxing and welcoming. Head Chef is also Exec
Chef for whole hotel group. Very involved in
local food industry. Modern British cuisine but
influenced by Chef's extensive travels. Open all
day with wide range of dishes. (Page 57)

Mark Napper, TRAWLERS ON THE QUAY
Buller Quay, East Looe, 01503 263593
Stunning harbourside setting. Take advantage of
Looe fish market on doorstep. Modern European
with Cajun influences. Menu changes daily to
take advantage of fresh catch. Interesting veggie
options. (Page 31)

Nick Tyler & Tom Pinch, TRENGILLY WARTHA INN
Nancenoy, Constantine, 01503 263593
Multi-award-winning inn in beautiful setting in a
wooded valley. Very varied bar menu catering for
all tastes (imaginative vegetarian options) with
many daily specials. Speciality wine list. Unusual
ales. Also dinner in the restaurant. *(Page 27)*

Garth Borrowdale
Previously of the award-winning Trehellas House
Hotel, Garth allows top quality ingredients to
speak for themselves in his globally inspired
dishes. *(Page 32)*

Paul Wadham, HOTEL TRESANTON
St Mawes, 01326 270055
*Olga Polizzi's stylish hotel at St Mawes has a stunning position looking out to sea over Falmouth Bay. Head chef Paul Wadham has worked at many top class restaurants and brings first class cuisine to Cornwall. Style is unfussy British - the best ingredients speak for themselves - but with a slight Italian influence. (**Page 37**)*

Kevin Viner, VINERS BAR & RESTAURANT
Summercourt, Newquay, 01872 510544
*Pioneer of quality food in Cornwall - first Michelin-starred chef in the county. Was UK National Chef of the Year winner in 1998. Viners awarded 'Bib Gourmand' by Michelin in 2005. Previous restaurants concentrated on fine dining but latest venture brings superb food in a relaxed and stylish setting at affordable prices. (**Page 44**)*

Mark Wishart
*Mark worked with John Burton-Race, Marco Pierre White (twice!) and Gordon Ramsey. Travelled the world, before settling in Cornwall previously at the Driftwood Hotel, Portscatho and his own restaurant in Truro. According to Mark, the secret is to use the best possible ingredients. (**Page 54**)*

For information about changes to Restaurant details see www.atmosphere.co.uk /cornishfood

Port Isaac Crab Tian with Cucumber & Brown Crabmeat Dressing

Ingredients ~
450g White hand-picked Crab meat
½ Cucumber peeled and thinly sliced
2 tsp White Wine Vinegar
100g Brown Crab meat
150 g Wild Rocket
Salt and Pepper
1 tsp English Mustard
¼ tsp Tabasco sauce
100 ml Sunflower oil
1 Lemon

Method ~ Put the cucumber into the vinegar and leave for 10 minutes.
Mix the brown crab meat with the oil, mustard and tabasco sauce and season to taste.
Take the white crab meat, season and add lemon juice to taste.
Use a mould about 4 inches across and spoon 2 tbsp of the white meat into the base. Then layer the cucumber (about 6-8 pieces) and another 2 tbsp of white meat.
Lift off the mould.
Dress the rocket with a little brown crabmeat dressing and arrange on top.
Spoon a little of the dressing around the dish.
Serve and enjoy.

Recipe by Ben Harmer
The Edge Bar & Restaurant - Port Isaac
Bookings - 01208 880090

St Ives

Constantine Bay Sunset

Bakehouse Summer Strawberry Cheesecake

Ingredients for Shortbread ~
100g Softened Butter
50g Caster Sugar
150g Plain Flour
Sprinkling of Caster Sugar for dredging

Ingredients for Strawberry Sauce ~
600g Fresh Cornish Strawberries
125g Caster Sugar
Juice of 1 Lime
Big sprig of fresh Mint

For the Mascarpone cream ~
Tub and a half of Mascarpone
250ml Strawberry sauce
1 Vanilla pod (seeded)
1 tbsp Icing Sugar

Method ~
Pre-heat the oven to medium heat (160^0-180^0C).
Put all ingredients for shortbread (except dredging sugar) into a mixing bowl and mix well with hands until texture resembles breadcrumbs.
Place on greased baking tray and bake until pale gold (10 mins). Re-crumble and bake for final 5 mins. Dredge in sugar.
Put all ingredients for strawberry sauce in pan and cook until soft but don't boil hard. Remove mint. Give a quick blitz in liquidiser and cool.
Whisk together mascarpone, vanilla and icing sugar. Stir in strawberry sauce. Fill piping bag (or spoon in carefully).

In champagne glasses layer the ingredients, alternating shortbread then mascarpone. Half way through add some strawberry sauce then repeat the alternating layers. Finish with more strawberry sauce and a sprig of mint.

Serve on a side plate with a few strawberries and a gert dollop of clotted cream!

Recipe by Andy Carr
Bakehouse Restaurant - Penzance
Bookings - 01736 331331

Serves 4

Tregothnan Tea Smoked Cornish Duck Breast

Ingredients ~
4 Cornish Duck breasts,
score the fat in a criss cross
pattern
Ingredients for smoking
mixture ~
200g Brown Rice
10g Tregothnan Classic Tea
1 Bay leaf, crumbled
1 Rosemary sprig
1 Garlic clove, crushed
Zest of 1 Orange

Method ~ Place all the ingredients for the smoking
mixture in the bottom of a large, deep frying pan and
slowly heat. Mix to avoid burning the edges. Place cooling
rack above the smoke mix and cover with a lid to increase
smoke density.
When the mix is smoking, place the duck breasts onto
the rack for 5 minutes then turn and smoke for a further 5
minutes. This will impart enough smoke flavour.
The duck is not yet cooked, so heat a dry frying pan on a
medium heat and place the duck breasts skin side down
and fry until the skin is crispy, turn over for a minute,
remove and put on a baking tray.
Place in a medium oven (160-180°C) for between 5 to 8
minutes until meat is cooked medium rare, depending on
size. Leave to rest in a warm place for 4 to 5 minutes.
Serve hot or allow to cool, slice and serve with salad and
some pickles.

Serves 4

Recipe by Anton Buttery
Langmans Restaurant - Callington
Bookings - 01579 384933

Lanyon Quoit

Port Isaac Crab Pots

Individual Potted Buttered Crabmeat

Ingredients ~
500g White Crabmeat
250g Brown Crabmeat
125g Unsalted Butter
½ tsp Cayenne Pepper
½ tsp Mace
2 tbsp Dry Martini
Pinch Salt
250g Salted Butter
1 tbsp Olive Oil

The simplicity of potted crabmeat suits a glass ramekin but you could use any small vessel, fancy mix and match coffee cups or tumblers, as long as they hold 5fl.oz.

Method ~ Make time to pick over the fresh white crabmeat carefully to ensure that no pieces of shell are inadvertently added to the finished dish and spoon into a mixing bowl. Put the brown crabmeat into the food processor or blender. Work until you have a smooth paste. Now add cayenne pepper, mace and martini and mix until completely smooth. Taste, season with salt and taste again. Then fold it into the white crabmeat using a metal spoon.
Melt the unsalted butter in a saucepan; switch off the heat and leave to cool.
Pour the cool butter onto the crabmeat mixture, then, still using a metal spoon, gently mix together. Spoon the crabmeat into the ramekins and using the back of the spoon, smooth the surface level. Place them in the refrigerator to set.
Melt the salted butter in a saucepan, add the olive oil and leave to cool and settle and separate. Have ready a jug, one large enough to allow a sieve to rest on top. Gently pour the melted butter through the sieve into the jug, leaving the watery liquid in the pan.
You need a thin layer of butter over the potted crabs to seal and preserve them. Spoon a little over and swirl each around so that the butter covers the top. Place them in the refrigerator to set. Covered with clingfilm they will keep for seven days.
Serve accompanied with warm crustless brown toast.

Recipe by Ann Long
The Rising Sun - St Mawes
Bookings - 01326 270233

Serves 8

Porthleven

Baked Cornish Squid with Arrabbiata Sauce, Roasted Cherry Vine Tomatoes, and Pangritata

Ingredients for Arrabbiata sauce~
1kg Beef Tomatoes, blanched, peeled & seeded
2 Cloves of Garlic, finely chopped
2 Chillies, halved & de-seeded
1 Small Onion, finely chopped

1 Kg of Cleaned medium Squid

Method ~ For the Arrabbiata~
Sweat off the onion and garlic in a little olive oil. When soft add the tomatoes and chilli and cook down gently until thickened to a sauce consistency.

Roasted Cherry Vine Tomatoes~ Take out the stalks of the tomatoes, place on a baking sheet and drizzle with the olive oil and sea salt. Pick the basil and cover the tomatoes with the stalks and reserve the leaves for later.

Ingredients for Pangritata~
200g of Dried Breadcrumbs
1 Clove of Garlic
1 De-seeded Chilli
300ml Olive Oil

Ingredients for Roasted Tomatoes~
500g Cornish cherry vine Tomatoes
Sea Salt
Olive Oil
100g Opal Basil

Place the tomatoes in a hot oven (approx. 200°C) for 10 minutes or until soft.

Pangritata~ Heat the olive oil and add the garlic clove and chilli to infuse. After a minute or so add the breadcrumbs and fry until golden. Drain.

Place the squid tubes and tentacles in a baking tray and cover with the heated arrabbiata sauce. Cover with foil and place in a moderate oven for 40 minutes or until tender.

Place the squid in a suitable bowl, pour over the remaining sauce, add the cherry tomatoes, dust with the pangritata and add the opal basil. Serve immediately.

Recipe by Neil Haydock
Fifteen Cornwall - Watergate Bay
Bookings - 01637 861000

Serves 6

21

Dawn on St Ives Bay

Baked Whole Sea Bass with Saffron and Lemon

Ingredients ~
1 Whole Sea Bass (450-675g gutted & de-scaled)
1 Lemon
½ a Large Onion
2 Pinches of Saffron
Splash of White Wine
Knob of Butter

Method ~ Firstly prepare the foil parcel, by folding the foil to double thickness - the parcel should be approx 4 inches longer and six inches wider than the sea bass. Lay the gutted and de-scaled sea bass in the centre of the parcel.

Soften the onions over a medium heat with butter, lemon and saffron. Stuff the sea bass with the filling and add a splash of good quality white wine.

Gather the foil at the top of the fish to form the parcel, but leave enough room for the fish to steam.

Place on a baking tray and cook in the centre of a moderately hot oven (190°C) for 20 minutes.

Serve with seasonal veg

Serves 1 hungry person!

Recipe by Daniel Zackey
The Mill House Inn - Trebarwith, Tintagel
Bookings - 01840 770200

Fried Green Tomatoes with Hand-Picked Cornish Crab & Cheat's Lemon Saffron Aioli

Ingredients ~
Salt & Pepper
3 cups of All Purpose Flour
I cup of Polenta
2 Large garden-fresh green Tomatoes
2 Cups of Egg Wash (Equal parts Egg and Milk)
2 Cups of Canola Oil

½ Cup Mayonnaise
Juice of 1 Lemon
1 Pinch of Saffron
1 tsp Sugar
1 Garlic clove, finely chopped
400g Fresh hand-picked Cornish Crabmeat
Pea shoots for garnish

Crab & Cheat's Lemon Saffron Aioli ~
Mix together mayonnaise, lemon juice, saffron, sugar and garlic. Fold the crabmeat into the mayonnaise mix, being careful not to break the crab up too much.

Presentation ~ Place 2 tomato slices on each of 4 plates. Top each with crab mayonnaise mixture. Garnish with pea shoots and serve.

Method ~ Fried Tomatoes ~
Add salt and pepper to 2 cups of flour. Mix remaining flour with the polenta. Slice tomatoes giving 8 thick slices, then dredge each in the seasoned flour then the egg wash, and finally in the polenta mixture.
Fry in canola oil until golden brown.

Serves 4 as a starter

Recipe by Grady Boone
Revival - Charlestown Harbour
Bookings - 01726 879053

St Michael's Mount

Great Flat Lode

Goat's Cheese and Herb Souffle

Ingredients ~
25g Unsalted Butter
30g Plain Flour
150ml Milk
3 Large Eggs plus 2 extra Egg
whites

25g Grated Cheddar Cheese
25g Goat's Cheese
Salt and Pepper to season
50g of Chopped Parsley, Dill,
Chervil

Method ~ You will need a soufflé dish measuring 14 cm diameter although you could get away with anything similar. Pre-heat the oven to gas mark 6, 200°C.

Separate the eggs so you have the yolks and the whites in different bowls. Melt the butter in a pan, then add the flour and stir until it thickens. Simmer for a few minutes making sure to stir to ensure it doesn't burn.
Next add the milk to the mixture bit by bit and stir until it has become thick and smooth, just add a pinch of salt and pepper.

Combine the egg yolks with the white sauce. Add the goat's cheese, cheddar cheese and herbs and mix everything together thoroughly.
Next take the separated egg whites and using an electric whisk switch it on to low and beat the whites for about 30 seconds until they begin to start foaming, then increase the speed of the whisk to medium and then to high, moving the whisk round and round the bowl while it's beating until you get a smooth, glossy mixture that stands in stiff peaks when the whisk is removed from the bowl.

Next, using a large metal spoon fold the whisked egg whites in to the other mixture. Using cutting and turning movements fold the mixture together until everything is well amalgamated. Don't stir the mixture with the spoon – it must be folded. Try not to spend too much time on this. Do it as quickly as you can to make sure your soufflé turns out light and fluffy.

Pour into a greased and floured mould and bake in a bain-marie (a tray with water that comes about ¼ of the way up the dish) for 25-30 minutes. Make sure there is plenty of room above for the soufflé to rise. When it's done it should be nicely browned on top, well risen and beginning to crack.

Recipe by Nick Tyler and Tom Pinch
Trengilly Wartha Inn - Constantine
Bookings - 01326 340332

Serves 3-4

Cornish countryside near Bude

Marinated Wild Cornish Venison with a Brandy & Red Wine Sauce

Ingredients ~
4 Venison steaks (Cornish if available)
2 Carrots
1 Onion
2 Sticks of Celery
2 tbsp of Brandy (approx)

Approx ½ bottle Red Wine
Nutmeg
Salt
Pepper
4 Bay leaves
3 Sprigs of Thyme
½ tbsp Olive Oil

Method ~
Trim the venison of any fat and sinew.
Season the steaks with the nutmeg, salt and pepper.
Finely chop the carrot, onion and celery and place into a container large enough to hold the Venison steaks.
Sprinkle the chopped vegetables with the crushed bay leaves and sprigs of thyme.

Add venison steaks to the vegetable mix covering as much as possible.
Pour the brandy and red wine over the vegetables and steaks ensuring the steaks are just covered.
Cover with cling film or a lid and refrigerate for at least one hour, more if possible.
When the Venison has been marinating for long enough, put the olive oil into a frying pan and heat until quite hot. Remove the steaks from the marinade and place into the hot oil. Fry the steaks as you would for sirloin or to your liking, bearing in mind that the more you cook the steaks the tougher they will become.
Just before serving add to the pan the juices from the marinade and allow to simmer.
Place the steaks onto serving plates and pour over the sauce from the pan. Enjoy.

At the restaurant this is quite a favourite. We serve it with wild mushrooms fried off with a little garlic, chilli and lemon juice.

Recipe by Nigel Parry
The Beach Restaurant - Sennen Cove
Bookings - 01736 871191

Serves 4

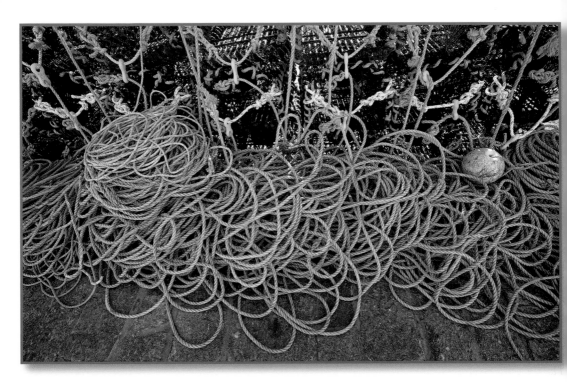

Crab Pots at St Ives

New Orleans Style Cornish Seafood 'Gumbo'

The Roux (what we use to thicken the Gumbo)~
150ml of either Olive or Vegetable Oil
75g Plain Flour
Place the flour on a baking tray in a pre-heated oven (160-180°C) for around 15 mins until it is golden brown.
Combine the flour and oil in a non stick pan and cook over a medium heat for 3 to 4 mins - place to one side.

For the Stock~
2 tbsp of Olive Oil
2 Large Onions, finely chopped
2 Cloves Garlic, finely chopped
4 Spring Onions, finely chopped
2 Chopped Peppers (one green and one red)
1 to 2 Finely chopped fresh

Chillies - according to 'heat' required
3 large Tomatoes, finely chopped
3 Sticks Celery, finely chopped
1 tbsp Sea Salt
2 tsp 'Cajun' spices (avail at most delicatessens & supermarkets) or you can use cayenne pepper or paprika instead - the former is 'hotter'
1/2 tbsp of Ground Black Pepper
5 Bay leaves & 1 tbsp each of chopped fresh Basil, Thyme and Oregano
2 litres of Fish Stock (preferably prepared by yourself, although you can buy powdered fish stock)
1 tbsp of Worcestershire sauce
1/2 tsp Tabasco sauce - phew !

Method for the stock~ Heat the olive oil in a large pan. When hot add the onions, celery, garlic and peppers and sauté gently for around a minute. Add the salt and pepper and sauté again for around a minute before you add the roux and cook for 5 minutes, stirring occasionally. Now add all the other ingredients and cook on a high heat for around 10 minutes, before cooking for a further 15 minutes on a low heat.

When you are ready to serve the dish, place the stock in a large saucepan, bring to the boil and then add
75g of Fresh Cornish Crab meat,
75g of Peeled Prawns,
75g of Chopped mixed Cornish Fish (you can use Cod, Monkfish or any White Fish), and finally add
10 to 20 fresh Fowey River Mussels or Cornish Clams.
Cook on a medium heat for about 10 minutes.
Serve in a large bowl and garnish with freshly chopped parsley.

Recipe by Mark Napper
Trawlers - Looe
Bookings - 01503 263593

Serves 8-10 as a starter, 6-8 as a main course with rice

Mediterranean Prawns with Leek, Dill & Cornish Yarg Cheese

Ingredients ~
225g Prawns
110g Cornish Yarg Cheese
250mls Creme Fraiche
1 Large Leek

¼ Cucumber
25g Fresh Dill
25g Butter
125-175g Basmati Rice

Method ~ Bring a pan of salted water to the boil and cook the basmati rice, this should take 10-15 mins. Finely chop and wash the leek. Melt the butter in a medium sized saucepan and saute the leek with the fresh dill. Season well. Dice the cucumber leaving the skin on and grate the Cornish yarg cheese including the nettle rind.
Check the rice. When it is cooked but still has a bite, drain well and keep warm. Add the creme fraiche to the leek and bring to near boiling point. Add all the other ingredients and stir frequently to prevent sticking. Cook for 8-10 mins for the prawns to cook through, the Cornish yarg cheese to melt and the cucumber to soften. Serve at once on a bed of drained basmati rice.

Serves 2 - 3 as a main course, 4 as a starter

Recipe by Garth Borrowdale

The Coast at Kynance

Local Hake Poached in a Saffron Stock served with Creamy Mash & Mussels

Ingredients ~

1-1.5kg Hake (ask your fishmonger to fillet & trim but keep the bones & trimmings)
500g Bag of Mussels
2 x 125ml White Wine (we use Camel Valley Atlantic Reserve)

100g Butter
750g Potatoes (good mashers we use Caesar)
50g Clotted Cream
6 Peppercorns
1 Onion
Parsley stalks, Bayleaf & a sprig of Thyme
Pinch of Saffron

Method ~ Cut 2-3 square portions from each of the 2 hake fillets; set aside on a plate for finishing in fridge.

For the Stock ~ Finely chop the onion & place with 25g of the butter in a large saucepan. Add the peppercorns, parsley stalks, bayleaf & thyme. Cook without colour for 5 minutes. Add all the hake bones & trimmings. Fry for a further 5 minutes. Add 1½ glasses white wine & 2 litres of water. Bring to the boil & simmer for 20 minutes, skimming off any fat or scum. Strain and reduce to a ⅓ of original volume. You should be left with 850ml.

For the Mussels ~ Place the mussels in a sink full of cold water. Any that are open tap on the side of the sink, if they don't close discard them. The rest, scrape the shells clean and pull off the beards. Again set to one side for later use.

Make a creamy mash (need I really say more?) ~ Peel the potatoes. Cook in boiling salted water. Strain & mash. Season & add clotted cream & butter.

To assemble the dish place the stock, white wine & saffron in a large wide bottomed pan. Add the squares of hake and cover with the mussels. Put a lid on top. Bring to the boil and cook for 3-4 minutes until the mussels just open and the hake should be just cooked (firm to the touch when pressing with a finger).

Place the hot mash in the centre of each plate, ring with mussels & crown with the hake. Drizzle a little of the saffron stock over & around.

Recipe by Keir Meikle
The Navy Inn - Penzance
Bookings - 01736 333232

Serves 4 - 6

Day Boat leaving Looe

Mevagissey Fishing Boats

Falmouth Bay Scallops - simply done

Ingredients ~
16 Fresh Scallops
Pinch of Malden Sea Salt
Twist of ground White Pepper
1 tsp of Olive Oil

Sauce ~
1 tsp of White Wine Vinegar
2 tsp of White Wine
2 Medium Shallots, finely chopped
1 tsp of Double Cream

200g Cornish unsalted Butter (diced)
1 tbsp Grain Mustard
Salt and pepper

Garnish ~
12 Cornish Asparagus Spears (peeled and blanched)
1 Bunch of Chervil

Method ~ In advance, prepare the sauce

Bring the white wine vinegar, white wine and shallots to the boil. Add double cream & return to the boil. Add the butter slowly and continually stir, do not allow to boil. Add grain mustard, salt and pepper and keep warm until required.

Heat a grill pan. Lightly oil the scallops and season. Place the scallops onto the grill pan and allow to colour, then turn them over and repeat until just cooked.

Arrange the scallops on a suitable plate, drizzle with the mustard butter sauce and arrange asparagus and chervil leaves to garnish.

Recipe by Paul Wadham
Hotel Tresanton - St Mawes
Bookings - 01326 270055

Serves 4

Pencarrow Head

Compote of Dried Fruit with Warm Gingerbread

Ingredients for Gingerbread ~
225g Butter
225g Soft Dark Brown Sugar
350g Plain Flour
2 Eggs, beaten
2 level dsps ground Ginger
2 level dsps ground Cinnamon

1 pinch Salt
2 level tsps Bicarbonate of Soda
275 ml warm Milk
225g Black Treacle

Method for Gingerbread ~
Heat oven to 150⁰C.

Grease and line a tin with greaseproof paper. Slowly melt together the treacle, sugar and butter stirring consistently. Remove from the heat and stir in the beaten eggs. Sieve the flour, salt, cinnamon and ginger and stir into the melted mixture. Sieve the bicarb into a separate bowl and pour the warm milk on to this and mix well, then add this to the treacle mixture. Give a good mix, stirring well and pour into your lined tin. Bake for 1½ hours. Leave to cool slightly before turning out on to a cooling rack.

Method for Fruit Compote ~
Soak a selection of preferred dried fruit overnight in water: pears, prunes, dates, pineapple, raisins, apricots to name a few. Make a stock syrup of 225g of granulated sugar to 325 ml of water. Dissolve the sugar in the water and bring to the boil. Take off the heat and add 1 vanilla pod split lengthways, 2 cinnamon sticks, 1 star anise and the peel of 1 orange and 1 lemon. Bring gently back to the boil and add the drained dried fruit. Simmer for 15 mins. If adding dried dates it is best to add these right at the end to avoid them breaking up.
Either jar the fruit or put into an airtight container in the fridge.

To Serve ~
Slice a generous portion of gingerbread and warm in the oven. Take a good large spoon of the compote, not forgetting the syrup and place the warm gingerbread to the side with a dollop of clotted cream or cinnamon ice-cream. Lovely!!!!

Serves 8

Recipe by Paul Ripley
Ripley's Restaurant - St Merryn
Bookings - 01841 520 179

Bude Bay Mackerel, Potato, Beetroot, Caper and Bacon Salad

Ingredients ~
900g Mackerel, filleted & pin boned
225g Cornish New Potatoes, cooked, peeled
& cut into 1cm dice
2 tbsp Good Mayonnaise
2 tbsp Herbs, finely chopped (Chives,
Tarragon, Dill or a mixture)
1 Lemon
½ Red Onion, finely chopped
2 Pre-cooked Beetroot, finely sliced
2 Sprigs of Thyme
12 Caper berries or a handful of baby
Capers
4 Rashers of Streaky Bacon
Handful of bitter leaves such as Frisee or
Rocket
Sea Salt and White Pepper
Light Olive Oil
Knob of Butter
Plain Flour (optional)

Method ~ Marinate the beetroot with a little olive oil, thyme, salt and pepper a couple of hours in advance. Mix together the potatoes, mayonnaise, herbs, red onion, half the juice of the lemon and salt and pepper to taste. Grill or bake the bacon until very crispy, set to one side. Divide the potato salad on to four plates, making a small pile in the middle and arrange four or five slices of beetroot on top. Season the mackerel and place in the flour skin side down, patting off any excess flour. In a medium hot non-stick pan, put a splash of olive oil and a knob of butter and when foaming add the mackerel skin side down and cook gently for 2 minutes.
Meanwhile dress the salad leaves with a little olive oil, lemon juice and salt and pepper. Then put a small pile on top of the beetroot and scatter each plate with the capers. Flip the mackerel over and remove from the heat. Add a splash of lemon juice and a knob of butter and baste the mackerel. Remove on to kitchen paper then place on top of the salad.
Finally, finish with the crispy bacon and a drizzle of lemon and olive oil.

Recipe by Kyan Hooper
Elements - Bude
Bookings - 01288 352386

Sea Thrift near Port Gaverne

Trevethy Quoit

Line Caught Cornish Sea Trout Sashimi with Soy Mirin Dressing and Wasabi

Ingredients ~
1 Side of Sea Trout, trimmed and pin-boned
(use the middle piece for the best results)
1 Tube Wasabi
1 Small jar Pickled Ginger

For the Marinade~
½ tbsp White Sugar
1 tbsp Sea Salt
3 tbsp Mirin

For the Dressing~
⅓ Cup Mirin
⅓ Cup Soy Sauce
2 tbsp Rice Wine Vinegar

For the Garnish~
80g Mizuna (or Rocket) leaves
Chopped Chives

Method ~ Rub trout with marinade half an hour before you serve it. Mix together the ingredients for the dressing.

To Serve ~ With your sharpest and thinnest blade, slice trout into 1½ mm thick slices.
Arrange on platter and pour over the soy mirin dressing. Form mizuna/rocket into a ball in the middle of the platter.
In a dipping bowl squeeze out some wasabi, add pickled ginger and some soy mirin dressing or soy sauce.

Recipe by Jude Kereama
Kota - Porthleven
Bookings - 01326 562407

Twice Baked Cornish Cheese Souffle

Ingredients ~
450ml Milk
Slice of Onion
Pinch of Nutmeg
75g Butter
75g Flour
Pinch of dry English Mustard
250g Menallack Farmhouse Cheese, grated
6 Eggs, separated
Salt
Pepper
450ml Double or Whipping Cream

Method ~ Butter the insides of 8 teacups.
Heat the milk slowly with the onion and nutmeg. Remove the onion. Melt the butter and stir in the flour and the mustard. Add the milk, off the heat, whisking until the mixture is smooth. Return to the heat and bring to the boil, stirring all the time. When thickened, remove from the heat and add 225g of the cheese. Stir in the egg yolks and check the seasoning. Whisk the egg whites until stiff and fold into the cheese mixture.
Fill the teacups two-thirds full with the mixture. Stand them in a roasting tin of boiling water and bake at 190°C for 15-20 minutes until set.

Allow to sink and cool, then loosen the souffles and turn them out into a buttered ovenproof dish.
Heat the oven to 230°C. Sprinkle the remaining cheese over the top of the souffles and coat them with the cream, seasoned with salt and pepper. Bake for 15 minutes or until risen and brown.

This dish makes an excellent starter or light lunch dish with salad and crusty bread.

Chef's Note: The souffle can be made with any firm cheese at the first stage. When you re-bake it, a mixture of grated cheese and any Cornish cheese may be used. Also, either sliced spring onions, roast red peppers or celery with walnut can easily be added to give you a choice.

Recipe by Kevin Viner
Viners Bar and Restaurant - Summercourt
Bookings - 01872 510544

Serves 8

Coastline near Lizard Point

Goat's Cheese and Sun-Dried Tomato Quiche

Ingredients ~
200g Plain Flour
75g Butter
50g Margarine
2 Egg yolks
60ml Water
Approx. 150g Goat's Cheese
2 Red Onions, thinly sliced
and caramelised in butter

Sun-dried Tomatoes to
taste, sliced
140 ml Cream
140 ml Milk
1 Egg yolk
1 Egg

Method ~ Place flour, butter and margarine in a mixing
bowl and work into a fine crumb. Add the beaten egg and
then the water. Do not overwork. Chill in fridge if prefer.
Roll out the pastry and line a buttered quiche tin. Prick the
pastry all over and cook for 15 mins at 190°C until lightly
brown. Brush all over with a little of the beaten egg and
return to the oven for a further 5 minutes. Leave to cool.
Crumble the goat's cheese and scatter together with the
sun dried tomatoes and caramelised onion in the pastry
cases. Mix the cream, milk and eggs together and season
if required. Pour the custard over the filling. Cook in the
oven for approx. 35 mins. until set and brown on top.

Makes two 7" quiches

Recipe by Tony Henshaw
The Eden Project - Bodelva
Bookings - 01726 811908

Dawn In the Cornish countryside

St Mawes

Crispy Skin Sea Bass with a Crunchy Thai Style Salad, Cornish New Potatoes and a Sesame and Soy Dressing

Method ~ Take the 2 large fillets of Sea bass and cut each fillet into two pieces. Working with the skin up, cut into the skin with a very sharp knife about a third of the way into the fish, set aside. Meanwhile, put 250ml of rice wine into a heavy bottomed pan and put on the heat; when the wine is boiling add the juice of one lime, 100ml of light soy sauce, 50 ml of honey, finely diced ginger and some sesame seeds, boil vigorously until a sauce consistency is achieved.

To make the salad simply shred bok choi or pak choi, white cabbage, red onion and coriander and dress it with a little sesame oil and lemon juice.

To cook the fish, heat a heavy bottomed frying pan, add a splash of olive oil and a light sprinkling of sea salt (this helps make the skin crispy). Gently place the fish skin side down and cook for 3-4 mins until the skin is golden brown and crispy; then turn the fish over and cook for a further 2 mins (or longer depending on how thick the fillets are when cooked). Place the fish somewhere warm.

To put the dish together, first put some buttered hot new potatoes onto a plate, place the salad on top of them and finally place the bass gently on top; then drizzle the soy and sesame dressing around the plate. If you have any coriander left finely chop it and scatter around the plate.

This dish is excellent as a starter or as a main course and eats very well at both lunch and dinner. It goes very well with a chilled glass of Camel Valley's 'Cornwall.'

Recipe by Paul McKenna
Fistral Blu - Newquay
Bookings - 01637 879444

Serves 4 as a main course, 6 as a starter

Chargrilled Wild Seabass with a Mussel & Saffron Vinaigrette

Ingredients ~
150-175g Wild Seabass fillet

Vinaigrette~
1 Shallot finely chopped
3 Saffron strands
1 Plum Tomato de-seeded
& cut into small dice
12 Mussels steamed and
taken out of the shell

Small bunch of Chives,
finely chopped
1 tsp White Balsamic Vinegar
1 tsp of the Mussel steaming
Liquor
Maldon salt and pepper to taste
2 tblsp Lemon oil

Method ~ Mix together all the above to form the dressing.

Heat your char grill pan until smoking hot.
Brush the seabass fillet lightly with oil and place across
the char grill bars for 2-3 mins until the skin becomes
crispy (do not lift off the grill during this time).
Season with salt and pepper.
Turn the seabass over and cook for a further 2 mins
depending on the thickness of the fillet.

To Serve ~
Arrange your vinaigrette in the centre of the plate and
drizzle a little around the plate. Place the seabass, skin
side up in centre of plate. Serve with wild roquette salad
and new season Cornish potatoes.
Very good with a glass of Spanish Albarino.

Recipe by Grant Nethercott
Alba Restaurant - St Ives
Bookings - 01736 797222

Serves 1

Cadgwith

Mevagissey Reflections

Baked Chocolate Pudding

Ingredients~
200g Best quality Bitter
Chocolate
200g Unsalted Butter
3 Whole Eggs and 3 egg
yolks
125g Caster Sugar
10g Plain Flour

Method~Buy the best quality chocolate you can find and try to get 70% cocoa content. Gently melt the chocolate in a microwave using lots of short bursts rather than one long one as it burns very easily. Now melt the butter and mix with the chocolate, set aside and keep warm.

In a mixer beat together the eggs, egg yolks and sugar to form a sabayon. (The mixture turns nearly white and resembles raw meringue.) Now using a hand whisk fold the chocolate mixture into the sabayon using a gently twisting motion, sieve the flour over the top of the mixture and very gently fold this in with a wooden spoon. Carefully butter and flour a ramekin and spoon in the mixture so it fills about three quarters of the dish. Now bake in a preheated oven set at 220°C for 11 minutes. When cooked, carefully release the pudding from the edge of the mould and turn out on to a warm plate. The pudding should be hot but runny in the middle. Serve with cream or ice-cream.

This recipe depends on the oven temperature and timings being precise. If it doesn't work for your oven, adjust the timing by 30 seconds and retry.

Recipe by Nigel Tabb
Tabb's Restaurant - Truro
Bookings - 01872 262110

White Chocolate Mousse with Raspberries

Ingredients ~
250g White Chocolate with Vanilla
170ml Milk
10ml Eau de vie framboise

1½ leaves Gelatine, softened
250ml Double Cream
Icing Sugar to taste

Punnet of Raspberries
Shortbread biscuit to serve

Method ~ Warm milk and pour over chocolate to melt. Dissolve gelatine in warm eau de vie, add to chocolate, mix & leave to thicken slightly. Whip cream to a soft peak. Gently fold in chocolate mixture and leave to set in fridge.

Marinate the raspberries - a variety called Glen Prosan is particularly good - in a splash of eau de vie. Puree some with icing sugar to taste, pass through a sieve and reserve.

To Serve ~
Arrange the raspberries on a shortbread biscuit, top with a quenelle of the mousse and pour sauce around.

Eau de vie framboise- similar to schnapps and available from all good wine merchants. A good vodka would make a decent alternative.

Recipe by Mark Wishart

Coombe Near Truro

Farmland near St Ives

Lightly Smoked Cornish Beef Fillet, Oxtail Faggot, Horseradish Scented Cauliflower Puree and Tribute Gravy

Ingredients ~
600g Cornish Beef fillet
2 cups Oak wood chippings
Seasoning

1 kg Oxtail, on the bone
25g Flour
50g Lard
4 Shallots, chopped
1 Clove Garlic
250 ml Beef Stock
250 ml Tribute Ale
1 Carrot
1 Bay leaf, sprig of Thyme

1 Savoy Cabbage
Seasoning

½ Leek, finely chopped
4 Shallots, finely chopped
1 Carrot, finely chopped
Tarragon
250 ml Tribute Ale

250g Cauliflower fleurets
250ml Chicken Stock
30g Unsalted Butter
5ml Double Cream
1 tbsp Horseradish Sauce
Seasoning

Method for Oxtail Faggots ~ Trim oxtails and flour all over. Seal in lard in hob proof casserole dish. Add vegetables and brown all over. Add beef stock and ale, bring to boil, add herbs and place in oven for 4 hours at 185°C. Allow to cool slightly, remove meat and roughly chop. Pass liquid through a fine sieve. Blanch savoy cabbage leaves and refresh. Oil a ladle. Line with cabbage leaves, fill with the oxtail mix and wrap the leaves over to form the faggot.

Method for Tribute Gravy ~ Sweat off the vegetables and herbs. Add Tribute and reduce by ⅔. Add liquid from oxtails and reduce by ⅔ again skimming all the time. Pass through a sieve and set aside.

Method for Cauliflower Puree ~ Place cauliflower in chicken stock, bring to the boil and simmer until soft. Drain and puree with butter, cream and horseradish.

Method for Smoked Cornish Fillet ~ Place wood chips in a deep tray, place wire rack over. Season the fillet. Heat the tray until the wood begins to smoke. Turn down the heat and place the fillet on the wire rack. Cover tightly with foil and place in oven for 3 mins (190°C). Remove from oven and allow to cool, leaving covered. Seal fillet all over in the hot oil for 3 mins. Transfer to oven for 8 mins. Allow to rest before carving.

To Serve ~ Warm faggots in oven for 3 mins. Spoon cauliflower puree onto plate. Draw spoon through the puree to form a teardop shape. Carve beef onto centre of plate. Top with oxtail faggot. Drizzle Tribute gravy over faggot and around plate.

Recipe by Dez Turland
The Terrace Restaurant, Royal Duchy Hotel - Falmouth
Bookings - 01326 313042

Serves 4

Cornish Pilchards in Parmesan Batter with Honey-Dried Olives, Red Pepper Relish and Lemon

Ingredients ~
6 of the Freshest Cornish Sardines (scaled, gutted, heads removed)

For the Batter~
3 Free-range Eggs
1½ Cups of Reggiano Parmesan
3 Boquerones (Spanish white Anchovies)
1 tbsp Parsley, roughly chopped
Cracked Black Pepper

For the Pepper Relish~
2 Semi-dried Tomato brunoised
1 Roasted Red Onion
2 Roasted Red Peppers
1 Lemon segmented
Juice of 1 Lemon
Juice of 1 Lime
60ml Olive Oil
Fresh Coriander & Flat Leaf Parsley

Olives & Honey

Method ~ Begin the night before and dry the olives on a tray, drizzled with honey, in a cool oven (30°C) overnight.

Make the pepper relish: mix the finely chopped tomato, red onion and peppers together with the rest of the ingredients and season to taste.
Make the batter: break the eggs and whisk together. Add the finely grated parmesan, chopped anchovies, pepper and parsley. Dip the sardines in the batter and pan fry until golden.

Serve the sardines with a good handful of fresh Rocket leaves, the honey dried olives and red pepper relish.

Serves 3

Recipe by Michael Smith
Porthminster Beach Cafe - St Ives
Bookings - 01736 795352

Coverack Harbour

Bakehouse Strawberry Martini

Ingredients ~
50ml Strawberry Vodka
25ml Fraise liquor
Squirt of homemade Strawberry sauce

To make the strawberry vodka simply take one punnet of fresh strawberries and put into a bottle of vodka. Place in freezer and leave for one week.

To make the strawberry sauce put 675g of fresh Cornish strawberries, 140g caster sugar, juice of 1 lime and a big sprig of mint into a pan and cook until soft but don't boil hard! Remove mint. Give a quick blitz in a liquidiser and cool.

To make the strawberry martini put a few cubes of ice into a cocktail glass to pre-chill it. Place all the ingredients in a cocktail shaker with lots of ice and shake for all you're worth. Drain into cocktail glass and serve on a balmy summer's evening.

Recipe by Andy Carr
Bakehouse Restaurant - Penzance
Bookings - 01736 331331

Pendeen Lighthouse

Porth Beach

Index of Food and Places

Beef Fillet	57		Bude	28
Cheese	44		Cadgwith	51
Chocolate	53		Constantine Bay	14
Crab	12, 19, 24		Coombe	55
Duck	16		Countryside	47
Gingerbread	39		Coverack	59
Goat's Cheese	27, 46		Farmland	56
Hake	34		Great Flat Lode	26
Mackerel	40		Kynance	33
Pilchards	58		Lanyon Quoit	17
Prawns	32		Lizard Point	45
Raspberries	54		Looe	35
Scallops	37		Mevagissey	36, 52
Sea Bass	23, 49, 50		Pencarrow Head	38
Sea Trout	43		Pendeen	61
Seafood	31		Port Gaverne	41
Squid	21		Port Isaac	18
Strawberries	15, 60		Porth	62
Venison	29		Porthleven	20
			St Ives	13, 22, 30
			St Mawes	48
			St Michael's Mount	25
			Trevethy Quoit	42

For information about changes to Restaurant
details see www.atmosphere.co.uk /cornishfood